Great Sex After 50!

Great SeX After 50!

And Other Outlandish Lies About Getting Older

John McPherson

**Andrews McMeel
Publishing, LLC**

Kansas City

Close to Home is distributed internationally by Universal Press Syndicate.

Great Sex After 50! © 2008 by John McPherson. All rights reserved. Printed in Singapore.
No part of this book may be used or reproduced in any manner whatsoever without written
permission except in the case of reprints in the context of reviews. For information, write
Andrews McMeel Publishing, LLC, an Andrews McMeel Universal company, 4520 Main Street,
Kansas City, Missouri 64111.

08 09 10 11 12 TWP 10 9 8 7 6 5 4 3

ISBN-13: 978-0-7407-7116-3
ISBN-10: 0-7407-7116-7

Library of Congress Control Number: 2007939010

Close to Home may be viewed on the Internet at
www.GoComics.com.

Visit *Close to Home* Web store at
www.closetohome.com.

E-mail John at closetohome@mac.com.

www.andrewsmcmeel.com

———— **ATTENTION: SCHOOLS AND BUSINESSES** ————

Andrews McMeel books are available at quantity discounts with bulk purchase for educational,
business, or sales promotional use. For information, please write to: Special Sales Department,
Andrews McMeel Publishing, LLC, 4520 Main Street, Kansas City, Missouri 64111.

Dedicated to old farts everywhere

The older generation fights back.

"His high school reunion is tomorrow."

"My name is Ron and I'm . . . I'm . . . having a birthday!"

"Arnie asked to receive his lump-sum retirement entirely in ones."

"Mr. Brown, we warned you that everyone responds differently to the medication. You've got to admit, you have grown lots of new hair."

11

Just to see the expression on their faces, store clerk Rodney Clatch liked to offer senior discounts to forty-something women.

Although she had had a few gray hairs in the past, Kay found this one particularly hard to accept.

"Let me know if you find a set of dentures in there, ma'am."

"It's Stephen King's latest book in
extra-large type."

"Ed is having a tough time adjusting
to retirement."

Larry Vulmer: The Comb-Over King

"You'll probably find this considerably
more strenuous than other treadmill
tests you've taken."

"Unfortunately, Carolyn, your body has
rejected your face-lift."

"That suit is called 'The Optical Illusion.'"

"We had your prescription made into a necklace so you won't forget to take your pills."

"According to the computerized fitness monitor,
you died 8½ minutes ago."

"The wind chimes were a retirement gift
for Steve when he left the sanitation
department last year."

"I'm sorry, Mr. Credley, but due to our truth-in-advertising policy, your request for a vanity plate reading 'BUFF-HUNK' has been denied."

"Aw, heck, that's nuthin'! One time I took on
four kids who were walking on the wall
of the fountain! Started waving ice cream
cones in my face . . ."

"I couldn't get all her candles on one cake,
so I had to add on."

As part of the hazing ritual at **Spring Meadow
Retirement Center**, each new resident is
required to do twenty-five shots of prune juice.

"According to our background check, you missed seven days of kindergarten due to illness. That puts you in our high-risk category."

"Just make sure the pacemaker is on the proper
setting and you'll be fine, Mr. Lusk."

"Oh brother, not another one! When are you
middle-aged guys going to wise up and stop
shoveling your driveways?"

"Mr. Stekson, we are very busy people. Do you want the finest hair-replacement procedure available or not?"

31

The Nordstats devise a subtle plan to force their newly returned adult son to move out.

"Look at those dang-fool teenagers,
wearing their pants hangin' down low like
a coupla idiots."

"Okay, Mr. Cynic! Twenty-two years and
four kids later, it still fits! Pay up!"

"Ya know, you're not exactly doing wonders for morale around her."

35

"Hey, Virgil, come here! Check out the
cheesy-looking toupee collection **El Dorko**
there is packing!"

The affordable and increasingly popular
face-lift clip.

"When I was a kid, we had to get up, walk clear across the room, and turn a dial on the TV whenever we wanted to change the channel."

Life with a chronic article-clipper

39

At the Hair Center for Men research laboratory

"So then I said, 'A simple procedure that will
give me better hearing than I've ever had,
and without the hassle of a hearing aid?!
Where do I sign?!'"

"Okay, everyone. Very funny. Vulture-shaped
Mylar balloons to circle my head. Ha, ha, ha."

43

"That's right! No huffing and puffing for thirty minutes on a treadmill. We've developed a new stress test that is faster and more accurate."

"He's recovering fine. The only problem is that when he hiccups, his pacemaker changes the channel on the TV."

Having spotted some acquaintances, Vera activates the Instant Grandchildren-Photo Display™ in her purse.

"When you notice yourself becoming forgetful, just give it twenty hard cranks and your memory should be sharp for a good two or three days."

"This'll just take a second. It was
my husband's last request."

49

"The gentleman at the end of the counter would like to buy you a round of high-blood-pressure medicine."

"Now *that* is what I call a successful
hip-replacement operation!"

Out of concern for the ninety-seven-year-old bride and groom's health, the wedding goers wisely threw the birdseed underhanded.

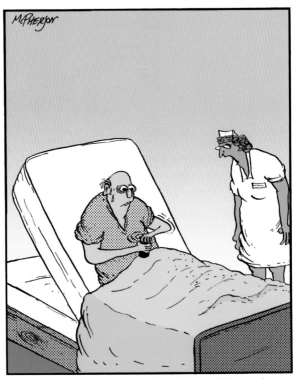

"Please keep trying, Mr. Fuller. We can't discharge you until you prove to us that you can open a childproof cap."

Disaster at the Rogaine plant

The agony of getting older

"It's called a phone booth, kids. Back in the days
before cell phones . . ."

58

59

"Well, her valves are shot and she's old so we'll never find replacement parts. Best thing to do is push her over the embankment out back and bury her."

61

"This isn't what I had in mind when I signed up
for the pet therapy program."

**Donna presents Kevin with his new
back-hair shaver.**

"For heaven's sake, will you just give it up and
admit that you need reading glasses!"

"Didn't you know? Today is Old Timer's Day
at the hospital."

With prescription drug costs skyrocketing, many senior citizens have come up with other ways to obtain their medications.

New in the fall TV lineup: *The Octogenarian Dating Game*

"Hey, Annette! Put this on! He should
be coming to any minute!"

"It's specifically designed to reduce the risk
of a heart attack."

"Oh, for heaven's sake, Larry! You forgot to take
off the price tag to your pacemaker!"

"Some men who go through midlife crises have affairs, some buy expensive sports cars, some climb mountains . . ."

Tired of constantly trimming his ear hair,
Steve tries to establish a new trend.

At GeezerDate.com

Overcome by curiosity, the Feelgemans open the door to the Trojan Horse and unwittingly allow their three grown adult children to move back home.

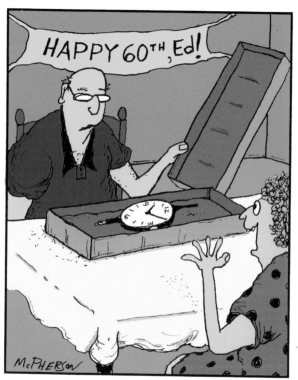

"It's a wristwatch designed so you can tell time without having to carry your reading glasses everywhere!"

**Mary's hot flashes were becoming
more and more intolerable.**

Though very pleased with her recent face-lift,
Gwen could no longer get her lips to touch.

"Mr. Simms, I think you have a very strong case for malpractice regarding your hip replacement."

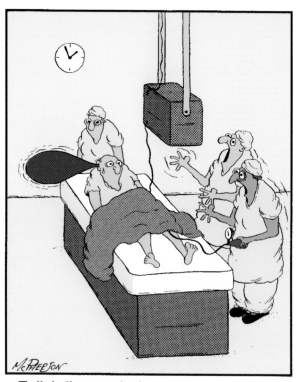

**Ted's balloon angioplasty procedure gets off
to a rough start.**